Also by Matt Forney

Available from Amazon.com and CreateSpace

Confessions of an Online Hustler

The Hitchhiking Crash Course

Trolling for a Living: The Best of Matt Forney, Volume One

Life During Peacetime

Big Lovin': The Guide to Picking Up Fat Chicks

Writing for Peanuts

Do the Philippines

by Matt Forney

Copyright © 2015 Matt Forney. All rights reserved.

ISBN-13: 978-1522791713

You can use short quotes from this book so long as you credit me. To use longer quotes, email me at the address below using subject line "Attention: Permissions Coordinator."

For further information, email me at admin@mattforney.com.

Cover design by Matt Lawrence of *MattLawrence.net*.

TABLE OF CONTENTS

Introduction	1
I: Welcome to the Philippines	5
II: The Girls	35
III: Game	53
IV: City Guides	76
V: Final Thoughts	83
Endnotes	86

ACKNOWLEDGEMENTS

First off, I thank the numerous men at Roosh V Forum and elsewhere for their guidance in helping plan my trip to the Philippines. In particular, I thank Mark Zolo of *NaughtyNomad.com* and 20Nation/Nicholas Jack of *SwoopTheWorld.com* for their encouragement and advice. I've included a list of references at the end of this book so readers can check out their perspectives on Filipinas.

I thank my editor and proofreader for giving *Do the Philippines* the once-over and getting rid of those nasty typos.

I thank my artist and graphic designer Matt Lawrence for his superlative work in creating the book's cover.

I thank Roosh V of *RooshV.com,* whose game advice not only helped me become decent with women, but whose *Bang* travel guides provided a template for this book.

Finally, I thank my friends Peter John McLean and Ann Sterzinger for providing the encouragement I needed to stop procrastinating and finish this damn thing.

DISCLAIMER

Remember, I'm just a guy on the Internet. While I've done my best to make this book as accurate as possible, to err is human and some of my suggestions either might not work for you or will become outdated in the years to come. Always do your own research before making any big decisions.

To Cheryl

I'm sorry I couldn't be the man you expected me to be.

INTRODUCTION

It was on a freezing November night two years ago in Manhattan's West Village that the seed of my Philippine adventure was planted.

I was on a pub-crawl with Mark Zolo, aka the Naughty Nomad, an Irish writer known for his exploits traveling the world and picking up girls. After ambling around the half-deserted streets, trading funny stories of our travels and getting ripped off on Bud Lights, we made our way to a quiet lounge bar near Jackson Square. I mentioned to him that I was considering going to Thailand, mainly because I wanted to start exploring the world and it seemed like a decent enough place to dip my toes.

"Don't go to Thailand," Zolo warned. "Go to the Philippines."

"Really?" I knew fuck all about the Philippines, aside from the fact that it was an American colony at one point. "What's the difference between Thailand and the Philippines?"

INTRODUCTION

"The Philippines is the easiest country to get laid in on Earth." Zolo spread his arms like he was bear-hugging Melissa McCarthy. "All the girls are sweet, speak English and they all dream of being married to a white guy. If you're making $1,200 a month from your blog, you can live there quite comfortably."

I didn't think much of it at the time. I was still living in upstate New York, still grinding away at my blog and books, socking away cash for some kind of getaway. Aside from brief visits to Buffalo for music shows, the New York City trip was the furthest I'd been from home since I came back from a cross-country hitchhiking trip to Portland, Oregon.

But Zolo's comments took root in my head, and as I plugged away at freelancing and blogging, my thoughts kept wandering back to the Philippines. I've never really had a problem with getting girls, but I've had trouble getting the girls *I* wanted. While I've never particularly cared for Asian girls, I'm also not willing to say no to a cute, feminine girl just because my little head has its own white hood and robes. Add in the truckloads of snow that bury Central New York in the winter and my desire to escape my dreary existence grew like a horny junior high schooler's erection in gym class.

As winter melted into spring, my cash flow increased to the point where I could finally spurn 9 to 5 employment

INTRODUCTION

and live solely off my writing. All the while, I kept researching what the Philippines were like; the girls, the laws, the weather, every detail a prospective love tourist would want to know.

Finally, in April of 2014, I was ready to take the plunge. I bought the plane ticket, rented an Airbnb apartment in Davao City, and got my shots at the travel clinic. It was time for me to see if the hype about the Philippines was true.

As it turns out, Filipinas were everything that Zolo had hyped them up to be and more. I spent three months in the Philippines—two months in Davao, one in Manila—and loved every minute of it. While there were many aspects of Filipino culture that grated on me, from the poor cuisine to the humid, sweltering weather to Filipinos' general lack of punctuality, I don't regret my trip one bit.

Regardless of how you feel about Asian girls, I recommend that every man visit the Philippines at least once. It's a place where you can effortlessly bang cute, pleasant girls who are eager to suck your cock *and* cook you dinner, but it's also a land where you can find a loyal, honest wife to bear your children. Whether you're looking to double, triple or even *quadruple* your notch count, or simply find a girl you can settle down with, Filipino girls have something to offer.

INTRODUCTION

However, don't expect to book a flight and immediately get a blowjob the minute you step off the plane. There are a *ton* of things you need to know about the Philippines before you go there, and if you aren't prepared to deal with the culture and the girls, they'll chew you up and spit you out. This book represents the sum total of my knowledge on the Philippines: dealing with the girls, getting transportation and lodging, and a whole lot more.

Let's dive in.

I

WELCOME TO THE PHILIPPINES

While I won't claim to be the most well traveled man—the only countries I've visited aside from the Philippines are Canada, Japan and Singapore—it's difficult to imagine any other nation coming close to the Philippines in terms of the sheer ease of pulling ass. Unless you have AIDS lesions on your face and/or are incapable of holding a conversation without yellowing your tighty-whities, it's impossible to *not* get laid here. In fact, I have no clue why the country has so many sex tourists throwing money at hookers when there are plenty of girls who will sleep with them for free.

Filipinas run the gamut from urban slut machines cruising FilipinoCupid for one-night stands with foreigners to sweet church girls who stay virgins well into their twenties, saving themselves for the right man. Most tourists only encounter the former because they stick to foreigner-infested sinkholes like Manila or Angeles City. However, if you're willing to visit out of the way towns such as Davao or Cagayan de Oro, you'll find the kind of girl that you'd be proud to make the mother of your kids.

Having said all that, the Philippines isn't some flawless paradise of sunshine and blowjobs. To begin with, the weather is not for everyone. Since the country's on the equator, expect year-round temperatures in the nineties and higher along with ball-blistering humidity. Leaving the house is like walking into an invisible swamp. Heavy rain is common, and typhoons are a regular occurrence throughout most of the country. I'm not a fan of tropical heat, so if you consider yourself more of a winter or autumn person, adjusting to the Philippine climate will take some time.

As a coda to the scorching hot weather, the air pollution in the Philippines is out of control. Because there are few (if any) controls on emissions, cars and factories belch out metric tons of particle-laden smog into the air. Portions of downtown Manila are so thick with smog that they resemble Los Angeles in the 1960's. Additionally, the air is thick with dust, meaning that if you have allergies or sensitive lungs, your first week in the Philippines is not going to be terribly pleasant. For example, I wear contacts, and my eyes actually began producing extra moisture as a response to all the dust and dirt blown into them on a daily basis. When I returned to the U.S. in October, my eyes had so thoroughly adjusted to the disgusting Philippine air that they kept producing extra moisture for a week afterwards, making me look like I was constantly on the verge of tears.

Second, the infrastructure in the Philippines is lacking. While far from the most poverty-ridden nation on Earth, Philippine cities have a haphazard and ramshackle design. It's common to find expensive, high-rise apartment buildings surrounded by an ocean of dingy tin shacks, like a game of *SimCity* being played by an Adderall-addicted fifth-grader. Most of Davao City's roads feature open running sewers and lack sidewalks, while Manila's roads are so poorly designed that there are minor floods after every rain shower. Power and water systems are barely functioning and can be knocked offline at a moment's notice, which is why most hotels and apartment complexes have backup generators. While Internet access and 4G phone service is available, speeds are inferior compared to first-world countries.

Finally, your final obstacle on the path to pussy paradise are the girls themselves. While Filipinas are every bit as cute and sweet as you'd think, they're far from stupid. Every Filipina has an inner predator, and if you don't know how to handle them, they will rip you apart. Additionally, due to the conservative nature of Filipinas outside the liberal megalopolises of Manila and Cebu, getting good girls into bed requires more time and work then you may be used to.

Because of this, if you're looking to slay some good girls and avoid the sluts and freelancers, you'll need to stay in one city for at least *one month* in order to truly enjoy the Philippines. If you have less than one month to spend on vacation, you're best served by going to Manila and focusing on one-night stands with loose girls. Given that it takes two or three dates to get girls from Davao and more conservative cities to warm up to you, if you don't have at least a month to spare, you won't have enough time to bang the girls you take out.

Fortunately, sealing the deal with Filipinas is ludicrously simple. If you can get laid in the U.S. (or Canada or whatever first-world country you're from), picking up Filipinas is like playing the game on very easy, with cheat codes enabled. Provided you have a bit of sack and aren't willing to tolerate bullshit, you'll also have an easy time dealing with the games Filipinas play.

Most guys who come to the Philippines stick to Manila or to sex tourist traps like Angeles City, then leave thinking that Filipinas are all craven prostitutes. The reality is that for all its pleasantness and promiscuity, there's a whole world of trustworthy Filipino girls who want to be wives and mothers. You just have to get away from the degenerate big cities in order to find them.

Philippine Culture

The Philippines has the (mis)fortune of being sandwiched in a strategic position in the Pacific, not far from China, Vietnam and Indonesia. Because of its location, the country has been invaded and colonized repeatedly by dominant regional powers, from the Spanish to the U.S. to the Japanese. Despite this, Filipinos don't have a chip on their shoulder regarding Americans or foreigners in general; in fact, according to the Pew Research Center's Global Attitudes Project, Filipinos feel more positively about America than Americans *themselves* do.[1] To this day, the U.S. and the Philippines retain close cultural and political links, and with China growing in power, the current Philippine president has sought closer military cooperation with America. Despite grinding poverty and repeated occupations by foreign empires, Filipinos are very outgoing and gregarious towards foreigners.

Indeed, Filipinas have a fetish for whiteness and white men that borders on creepy. While East Asians in general are fascinated with whites (skin-whitening cream is popular in Singapore and other Asian countries, for example), Filipinos take their obsession with whiteness to a whole other level. Filipinos who look white or European have greater social status than those who are more Asian or brown, as evidenced by the oddly Caucasian appearance of the nation's movie stars and pop singers. The average billboard in Manila or Davao City features models who are whiter than I am, and it's common to see girls using umbrellas when it's sunny out to preserve their pale complexions. Forget yellow fever: Filipino girls have "white fever."

While Filipino culture is far from intellectual, Filipinos take education seriously. Almost all of the Filipinas I dated and smashed were either in college or had already graduated. Given the strong influence that the Catholic Church has on Philippine culture (though this influence is weakening among richer youth), Philippine schools and universities aren't infected with the cultural Marxism and third-wave feminism that is tearing the West apart.

The main downside to Filipino culture is that it's really basic and unremarkable. While the openness and xenophilia of the average Filipino is definitely a plus, as it makes acclimating to the country a lot easier, they aren't terribly intellectual and are overly fixated on pop culture. In many ways, the Philippines feels like the U.S. circa the late 80's and early 90's. Culture revolves around malls (malls are incredibly popular in the Philippines), sappy love songs by Erasure and Air Supply dominate the airwaves, and American fast food franchises are ridiculously popular, sowing the seeds for an obesity epidemic a decade or two down the line. And karaoke. Dear God, do Filipinos love karaoke.

Additionally, Filipinos have only the loosest concept of punctuality. If a Filipino tells you he's going to meet you at noon, don't expect him to show until 1pm, maybe later. For example, when I was checking out of my apartment in Davao, the manager informed me that he'd be swinging by at 10am to settle my accounts. I had an interview with *Return of Kings* writer Quintus Curtius at 11am, so I figured I'd be done with the manager quickly. Nope: the manager didn't show until around 11:30, at which point I had given up on him showing and was already well into the Skype call with Curtius. I was forced to put him on hold and spent a good 20 minutes haggling with the manager, trying to determine whether I owed him money or he owed *me* money (my utility bills were being taken out of my security deposit), before I was able to get back on the phone with Curtius.

Other aspects of Philippine culture aren't really problems but can take some time getting used to. For example, whenever you go to a restaurant with table service, after you get your food, the waiter/waitress will almost *never* come back to check up on you; you have to pull them aside in order to get your check. Additionally, due to the huge population, labor is very cheap in the Philippines, so most retail businesses employ far more people than they actually need. For example, if you go to a fast food restaurant such as McDonald's or Jollibee (a Philippine-styled McDonald's knockoff), you'll have one employee take your order while you stand in line, another employee will ring you up, a third will bring you your meal, and a fourth will whisk away your trash when you're done. Even something as simple as going to the bathroom can trip you up; Philippine toilets are equipped with "bum guns," essentially handheld bidets that you use to clean yourself up after doing your business, and are *much* more sanitary than using toilet paper.

I'm not saying these things are necessarily *bad,* only that they're *different.* Despite their affinity for foreign cultures, Filipinos retain a unique character and way of viewing the world. Even if you're an experienced traveler, expect to suffer some culture shock when you touch down. For example, I spent much of my first day in the Philippines passed out in my apartment, both because I was severely jet-lagged (I left Chicago at nine in the morning on a Tuesday and arrived in Davao around noon on *Thursday*) and because I was overwhelmed by the alien nature of the people around me.

If you want a better handle on Philippine culture, I recommend reading the novel *Noli me tangere* by José Rizal. Rizal is one of the Philippines' national heroes: a journalist and nationalist, his execution in 1896 helped set off the Philippine Revolution and the Spanish-American War, freeing the Philippines from Spanish rule. *Noli me tangere* is considered one of the foundational works of Philippine culture in the same way that the *Iliad* and *Odyssey* are foundational works of Greek culture (or *Beowulf* is a foundational work of English culture), and reading it will give you some insights on the Filipino character.

Despite their obsession with pop culture and the ubiquity of smartphones, Filipinos are still more down-to-earth and humble than the average American. The Filipino personality is about living in the moment; since you don't know what tomorrow will bring, you might as well celebrate while you can. The downside of this mentality is that Filipinos don't think about the consequences of their actions very often, as evidenced by the country's ridiculously high birth rate and number of children born out of wedlock.

Additionally, despite what most people think, you do *not* need to learn Spanish to go to the Philippines. Following the Spanish-American War and the American occupation, English displaced Spanish as the preferred second language of Filipinos. English is one of the Philippines' two national languages (the other is Filipino, a standardized form of Tagalog), and because learning it is mandatory in schools, English fluency is virtually universal. In fact, because of the high rate of English fluency, many multinational corporations have started opening up call centers in the Philippines, and South Korean students form one of the country's largest tourist blocs, as learning English there is cheaper than doing it back home. While some Filipinos—particularly in cities with less tourist traffic—might be unfamiliar with American slang and catchphrases, it's possible to have a conversation with just about everyone you meet in the country. Because of this, there's no point in learning Filipino or any of the country's regional languages.

I'd like to end this section by discussing Philippine food and alcohol. When it comes to the former, just say no, at least when it comes to franchises and mall restaurants. Filipino cuisine is a freakish hybrid of Malaysian, Chinese and American cuisine, retaining pretty much all their bad aspects and none of the positives. As I mentioned already, American fast food chains such as McDonald's and KFC are growing in popularity, but local offerings such as Jollibee and Max's Restaurant aren't any better. When it comes to eating out, you're best off sticking to freestanding restaurants, so long as they look clean.

The imbibement of choice in the Philippines is beer, specifically the two biggest domestic brands: San Miguel and Red Horse. San Miguel is seen as being a bit classier, but Red Horse has a higher alcohol content—at 6.9% ABV—so you can get wasted pretty quickly on both. Both brands cost roughly 30-35 Philippine pesos (about $0.75 USD) a can at supermarkets. Strangely enough though, Filipinos don't drink too excessively when they're out, so you can save a bit of money when it comes to buying girls drinks.

The best way to describe Filipino culture is that it's like the katamari from *Katamari Damacy. Katamari Damacy* was a cult Japanese game from the mid-2000's in which you controlled an adhesive ball that sucked up everything it touched, slowly growing bigger along the way. Because of their history of being repeatedly invaded and colonized, Filipinos have developed a knack for adopting aspects of foreign cultures and making them their own. Because of this, you don't need to study Philippine culture that extensively in order to bang Filipinas. Once you've gotten over the initial culture shock, you'll adjust to their ways quickly.

Which Cities to Visit

The Philippines is a large country in both landmass and population. With 100 million people spread out across an archipelago of 7,000 islands, it's the 12th most populated nation in the world. While there are plenty of cities to visit, the most important ones for our purposes are the three largest: Manila, Davao City, and Cebu.

Manila—or more accurately, Metro Manila—is the capital of the Philippines and by far the most populated part of the country, with just shy of 12 million people. The region is an amalgam of several cities clustered together into one gigantic megalopolis, from Manila itself to Quezon City, Makati, Pasay and more. Because of its size and status as the country's capital, Manila is both culturally liberal and attracts a ton of tourist traffic. While I recommend spending a week or two in Manila just to get a feel for the place, I don't advise spending the entirety of your Philippine adventure there.

Manila has to be one of the easiest places to get laid on the planet. Despite the massive amount of tourists, the city's libertine atmosphere and the constant influx of Filipinos coming in from the provinces for work or school means there is a never-ending supply of cute girls looking to suck white dick. You won't get any bonus points for being foreign, but the girls are so slutty that it doesn't matter. However, I wouldn't recommend looking for a long-term girlfriend in Manila, because most girls there are sleeping around like crazy and a fair number of them even accept money for sex on the side (I'm not talking about prostitutes, of which there are plenty, but "normal" girls).

Additionally, Manila's size and status as the capital means that you'll never run out of ways to entertain yourself. The region has all kinds of scenes and neighborhoods, from the sleazy go-go bars and Korean-filled nightclubs of Malate to the posh, Manhattan-esque boutiques and lounges of Makati. You can also check out important tourist attractions such as Rizal Park, the National Museum of the Philippines, Intramuros and the University of Santo Tomas. Finally, Manila has some of the nicest malls I've ever seen (even by Philippine standards), most notably the Mall of Asia in Pasay and Greenbelt in Makati.

Next up is Davao, which is where I spent the bulk of my time in the Philippines. Davao is on the southern end of the island of Mindanao, best known in the U.S. for the ongoing civil war between Muslim separatists and the

Philippine government. Because of this, the State Department urges American travelers to avoid Davao and Mindanao in general, despite the fact that the civil war is happening on the complete opposite side of the island from Davao City. That's like urging people to avoid setting foot anywhere in Illinois because of gang shootings in the South Side of Chicago.

Davao is one of the safest cities I've ever lived in. Thanks to the efforts of Mayor Rodrigo Duterte, insurgents, drug smugglers and other miscreants stay far away from the city out of fear of getting a bullet in the brain. Not only is crime relatively low in Davao, the police and citizens are honest and helpful to foreigners. For example, I never once had a taxi driver try to rip me off, which Manila drivers would do to me *constantly*. Despite this, the cowardice of the average American means that foreigners are relatively rare in Davao, so your exoticness is much higher than in Manila. Expect to get stared at by Filipinos wherever you go; in fact, I was walking past a playground one day when all the kids suddenly stood up and started waving and cheering at me. I was probably the first foreigner they'd ever seen in their entire lives.

Davao's atmosphere is a world apart from Manila's. The city is very conservative, has an anemic bar and club scene, and girls are much less willing to sleep with you on the first date. I *did* get a one-night stand a couple days after coming to the city, but it was probably just beginner's luck, because it was the only one I got there. The advantage of the city's more reserved ethos is that you have a *much* better chance of finding a loyal girlfriend or wife than in Manila. Indeed, a significant percentage of the girls I banged there were either virgins or had only been with one other man before me.

The major downside to Davao is that there isn't much to do there. The city is lacking in museums and other touristy distractions, and the nightlife, as I mentioned, isn't much to write home about. Additionally, the city is dominated by fast food chains such as Jollibee, McDonald's, and Mang Inasal. When I wasn't either working, picking up girls, or going on dates, I spent much of my time in my apartment reading or playing video games because I was so bored.

The other major city of interest in the Philippines is Cebu. I didn't have time to visit it, unfortunately, so I can't give you specific pointers, but other men who've gone there describe it as being midway between the lustfulness of Manila and the conservatism of Davao. Additionally, there are a number of smaller cities such as Cagayan de Oro, Butuan and General Santos where your exotic factor will be off the charts.

Finally, while Angeles City is well known for catering to sex tourists, unless your goal is to sleep with prostitutes (and if it is, this isn't the book for you), I wouldn't recommend going out of your way to visit there. I had contemplated checking the place out for a weekend just to see what it was like (it's not far from Manila), but I didn't have the time. In addition, given the nasty reputation that Angeles City has, if you do decide to check it out, you're best off not telling any Filipina of quality unless you want her to write you off as a sleazy pervert.

Given the pleasant weather and huge population of the Philippines, you can go to any of these places at any time of year and bang girls. The only real consideration you need to take into account is typhoon season: while typhoons occur year-round, activity peaks between June and October. If you're worried about typhoons, you should avoid the Philippines during those months. Note that due to its isolated location on Mindanao, Davao rarely if ever experiences typhoons.

Logistics

Getting to and from the Philippines, while a bit more involved than other countries in Southeast Asia, is no challenge. Because the country is an archipelago, the most convenient way in is by air. Check websites like Skyscanner or Skiplagged for deals on flights, and expect to pay a bit more if you're flying to anywhere other than Manila. For example, a one-way ticket from Chicago to Davao City cost me just shy of $1,100, and it would have been about $150 cheaper if I hadn't waited to buy it until two months before I was leaving. A one-way return ticket to Chicago from Manila cost me 987 Singapore dollars (about $730 USD).

If you're looking for accommodation, you're best off going to Airbnb and renting an entire, fully furnished apartment. Quality hotels are not only considerably more expensive, they can actually hurt your success with girls because they'll assume you're a sex tourist. Renting an actual apartment will make it appear as if you intend to stay in the Philippines for the long haul, even if you're only there for a week. Additionally, don't ever waste your time with hostels because they're full of stupid white backpackers and typically ban you from bringing guests in. It's easy to find deals on Airbnb: for example, I stayed in a fourth-floor, one-room apartment in downtown Davao for roughly $450 a month; the building even had a swimming pool (one of the *easiest* ways to bang Filipinas) and an exercise room. If you're only staying in a city for a month or two, Airbnb will pretty much take care of your needs.

A close second option if you're only planning to stay in the Philippines for a short period is an *apartelle*. Apartelles are a cross between an apartment and a hotel: you get some of the amenities of a hotel (such as maid service), but apartelles cost less than apartments and don't require you to sign a lease. You can find apartelles in every Philippine city. For example, Jun 'N Dell Apartelles is a popular option in Davao: they charge between 18,000–20,000 pesos (about $380–425) a month.

If you're looking to stay in a particular city for six months or more, you may want to look into renting an apartment locally. A Google search for "city + apartment" (ex: "Cebu apartment") will return plenty of options. Please note that there are a *lot* of scammers looking to take advantage of gullible foreigners, so always investigate listings thoroughly and don't sign a lease that you aren't 100 percent comfortable with. For this reason, I recommend that even if you're planning a long-term stay in the Philippines, you should get an Airbnb rental or apartelle for at least the first month so you can search for a more permanent place at your leisure.

Finally, you should always keep in mind that the Philippines has a strong culture of bartering and haggling. When it comes to apartments and Airbnb listings, the price that's listed is *not* the price you have to pay; Filipinos not only expect you to try to haggle the price down, they'll think you're an idiot if you don't. You can give yourself discounts on accommodation by negotiating with the landlord: I managed to save about $75 a month on my Davao apartment this way.

When packing for your trip, you absolutely need to bring an unlocked smartphone. Cell phones are ubiquitous in the Philippines; virtually everyone communicates via text and even poorer people have flip phones. While you can get one-night stands easy in Manila, you'll need a phone if you plan on picking up girls any other way. The two major service providers in the Philippines are Globe and Smart, and you can obtain SIM cards at the airport for either one. I used Globe while I was over there, and their system is relatively simple: you purchase "load" (money) for your account, which allows you to make phone calls, text and use the Internet. Load cards in various amounts (100 pesos, 500 pesos, 1,000 pesos etc.) can be bought from Globe stores at malls. Word to the wise: if you plan to use 4G data with Globe, you should get one of their unlimited data plans so your phone doesn't end up eating your entire load. Check the Globe website for more info; the plan I used cost me about 1,000 pesos ($20) a month.

Additionally, if you need any other electronics (computers, tablets etc.), buy them *before* you come to the Philippines, because they're hellishly expensive there. For example, about a week into my trip, I dropped a $40 USB microphone on the floor and broke it. After frantically searching through every mall in Davao, I bit the bullet and purchased the only model of USB mic I could find, which cost me 12,000 pesos (about $250). Filipino electrical outlets are compatible with American plugs; however, the differing voltage and frequent brownouts means you'll be best off buying a surge strip when you arrive. You can get them at hardware stores in malls for about $10–15.

Finally, you need to bring your own condoms. No, I'm not joking. Because Filipinos' penises are smaller on average than whites' or blacks', the condoms sold in the

Philippines will be too tiny for you to use. While STDs such as HIV are not as common in the Philippines as they are in Thailand or other southeast Asian countries—and the good girls you'll meet in conservative cities like Davao are pretty much disease-free—you'll still want some rubbers to protect against pregnancies, particularly since abortion is illegal there. The U.S. and the Philippines don't have a child support extradition treaty, meaning that if you accidentally knock up a broad, you're home free so long as you get out of the country and don't come back, but I'm not comfortable leaving my child to be raised in a third-world slum. I recommend buying condoms in bulk online, because otherwise you'll run out of them in less than a week.

Generally, you should only bring as much stuff as you need. The more crap you bring, the more you'll stress out and the greater the likelihood that your things will be lost in transit and/or stolen. When I left for the Philippines, all I brought with me was a tiny carry-on suitcase and a computer bag. To further free up space in your suitcase, roll your clothes up into tight tubes instead of folding them: this compacts them and gives you more room.

As I mentioned earlier in the chapter, English comprehension is universal in the Philippines. While older Filipinos aren't as fluent as young ones and bilingualism is weaker in smaller, less-touristy cities, pretty much everyone you meet will be able to understand you. The only real changes you'll need to make to your speech are toning down your use of Western slang and ten-dollar words. Additionally, there are some quirks of Philippine English that take time to get used to. For example, Filipinos don't say "O" in place of "zero" in spoken English when it comes to long numbers, so if you read off, say, "103" as "one oh three," many Filipinos will have no idea what you're talking about; you have to say "one *zero* three" or "one hundred and three." Filipinos also have their own English-language slang; for example, "aircon" is their term for air conditioning. And if a Filipina calls you "gwapo" or "box office," it means she thinks you're handsome.

Ground transportation in the Philippines largely consists of taxis and jeepneys. Taxis are relatively cheap, particularly in smaller cities; I don't think I ever paid more than 250 pesos ($5) for a metered ride. Jeepneys are a cross between jeeps and buses and serve as the primary form of public transportation in most Philippine cities. Fares are based on how many blocks you travel. While jeepneys are cheaper than taxis, I rarely used them due to their lack of air conditioning. There are also intercity buses if you want to go between towns that are in the same vicinity, and Manila has its own light rail system. It's possible to rent a car if you have a driver's license, but it's not worth it: traffic in the Philippines is insanely bad, drivers are constantly hovering on the edge of homicidal, and having a car will make you a target of corrupt cops.

If you're looking for more information about the Philippines that isn't covered in this guide, I recommend checking out the *Roosh V Forum*. The "Travel" section has a wealth of knowledge about the Philippines and the guys there helped me out with many of the questions I had. The website *Live in the Philippines* is also a great resource. Finally, be sure to check out the sources I've listed at the end of this book, as they go into greater detail about the things I talk about here.

Entering and Exiting

Entering the Philippines is relatively easy: citizens from most Western countries (indeed, most countries period) are allowed up to 30 days of visa-free travel. Additionally, you can obtain visa extensions while in country. A 29-day extension costs 2,000 pesos (about $42) and you can extend your visa for up to two months at a time. Note that after you've been in the Philippines for 59 days, you're required to obtain a national ID card as well: it costs 3,500 pesos (about $74) and is valid for one year.

You can renew your visa at immigration offices in Manila, Davao and every other major city, a process that usually takes several hours. If you want to save time, go to a travel agency and have them handle the paperwork for you. For example, when it came time to get my visa extended, I went to Fast Pass Tours in Davao, which is on the same block as the city's Bureau of Immigration. For an extra 500 pesos ($10), I was able to get my visa extended and paperwork processed without having to sit around at immigration all day.

Additionally, in order to enter the Philippines, you *must* show proof that you will be leaving the country within the 30-day period in the form of a return flight. This requirement is not enforced by immigration itself—indeed, when I presented my passport to the immigration officer at the Davao airport, the only question he asked me was how long I was staying—but by the airlines themselves. Because the Philippine government levies heavy fines on airlines who allow passengers to board without a return flight, they will not allow you to get on the plane unless you show them proof of onward travel.

If you don't want to buy a round-trip flight, there's an easy way to get around this. Create a fake itinerary on Travelocity, Expedia or another similar website showing your return flight, and then email it to yourself so you can show it to the desk clerk on your phone. Zoom in on the screenshot so the portion of the itinerary showing that you *haven't* purchased the return ticket is out of view. The clerks are not going to scrutinize your itinerary; all they want to see is a return flight that they can punch into their computer. You can also print out the fake itinerary; use Microsoft Paint or another photo-editing program to erase the portion that says you haven't bought the return flight. Another solution is to purchase a cheap flight to Singapore, Kuala Lumpur or another nearby foreign city, then cancel it when you arrive in the Philippines.

Finally, when you depart the Philippines—or indeed, fly anywhere else in the country—you're required to pay a transit tax. The tax is 200 pesos ($4) for domestic travel and 550 pesos ($12) for international travel. Some airports, such as the Manila Ninoy Aquino International Airport, have started integrating the transit tax into ticket prices. Don't overstay your visa because when you go through the airport, you'll need to pass through immigration again if you're on an international flight, and you'll be heavily fined.

Safety

When I told my family that I was going to the Philippines, they all assumed that I would be robbed, killed and raped… in that order. I left the country safe and unharmed—aside from doing a few things that made me feel guilty afterwards—but that's primarily because I took precautions and didn't do anything stupid. If you don't want to end up dead in an alley, heed my advice.

To begin with, when you leave the house, only take what you need. Carrying around a backpack or computer bag will make you a target for muggers; this is why you'll see Filipinos wearing their backpacks backwards. Whenever I left my apartment, the only things I took with me were my wallet, house keys, smartphone and earbuds. When it comes to your wallet, leave your ATM card, credit cards, driver's license and other IDs at home unless you need them. Ideally, you should be carrying cash and nothing else, and even then, only carry as much cash as you'll need for drinks, dinner, taxis or whatever you're going out for. This ensures that even if you get robbed or pickpocketed, you won't end up losing everything. Finally, only take items out of your pockets when you need them; for example, don't carry your smartphone around in your hand when you're walking around snapping pictures.

To deter pickpockets, never put *anything* in the back pockets of your jeans. Avoid large crowds, and if you have no choice but to walk into a crowd, put your hands into your front pockets to protect your stuff. Don't assume that you'll be able to feel a pickpocket reaching his hand into your pants, because they've trained themselves to be invisible. While some men recommend using a dummy wallet to distract pickpockets while keeping the bulk of your cash in a neck wallet, I found that to be unnecessary. Additionally, try to avoid groups of beggars, and don't give them any money. While this may seem heartless—especially considering the levels of poverty you'll see—if you give money to a homeless person, you'll get mobbed by beggars looking for a handout.

At night, don't walk around shady nightlife areas, such as Manila's Malate district. Take taxis whenever you need to go somewhere distant. Don't get hammered, because predators absolutely love taking advantage of drunk foreigners. Stay aware of your surroundings and avoid groups of Filipino men. While I'm not opposed to drug use, carrying drugs is a *very* bad idea, because if a cop arrests you, you're looking at jail time and possibly worse. Drug smuggling in the Philippines is punishable by death; though the death penalty has been suspended since 2006, there's no guarantee it won't be reinstated. As I've said before, don't be a dumbass: you'll live longer.

Finally, beware of scams. For example, depending on where you are, taxi drivers will try to rip you off. The most common scam is that the driver will try to turn off the meter and charge you a much higher fare: for example, when I took a taxi from my Manila apartment to the airport, my driver tried to quote a price of 700 pesos when it would probably be only 400-500 on the meter. If a taxi driver tries to pull this scam on you, tell them to turn the meter on instead. If they refuse, get out. While the difference in cost isn't that huge by Western standards, there's no reason to let some scumbag gyp you. Taxi drivers trying to rip you off are rare in Davao—I never once encountered a driver who *didn't* use the meter—but are extremely common in Manila.

Another tactic I tried—one I borrowed from Roosh V—is to only ride taxis driven by middle-aged or older men.[2] Young drivers are more likely to rip you off, while older married guys don't have the energy to swindle foreigners. They just want to put in a day's work and go home to their wife and kids.

In general, while the Philippines can be dangerous, these tips will save your bacon in most cases. Unless you're specifically looking for trouble, you'll be fine provided you take the necessary precautions. For more up-to-date information, check out the State Department website as well as travel forums.

Health

While hygiene and public health in the Philippines is lax compared to the West, you won't have to worry about your ass constantly spewing fecal soup provided you stay smart.

To begin with, before you leave the country, make an appointment with a travel clinic to get the necessary shots. The CDC recommends getting vaccinated for hepatitis A and typhoid because they are easily transmitted through food and water. In particular, the hepatitis A vaccine is administered in two stages: an initial shot that gives you immunity for six months, and a booster shot that confers lifetime immunity. Because hepatitis A and typhoid have virtually been eliminated in the West, most hospitals and healthcare providers don't administer them, so you'll need to visit a travel clinic.

The CDC also recommends staying on guard against hepatitis B, Japanese encephalitis, malaria and rabies. You've likely already been vaccinated against hepatitis B (I received the shots when I was a kid), and even if you aren't, unless you're planning to shoot up with dirty needles and/or have unprotected sex with prostitutes, it's not really a big concern. You can avoid rabies by staying away from the hundreds of stray cats and dogs that wander the streets of Philippine cities; while most travel clinics provide rabies shots, they cost hundreds of dollars and are administered over the course of a month. Malaria and Japanese encephalitis are only a problem if you plan to spend a lot of time in the jungle; deterring mosquitos by wearing long-sleeved shirts and pants and using insect repellent is all you need to do.

Ironically, the only diseases I had to worry about when I was in the Philippines were the same ones I had to worry about back in the U.S.: the common cold and the flu. My ethnic background is largely northern European (French, English, northern Italian, and Polish) and didn't cotton to the Philippines' triple-digit temperatures and bog-like levels of humidity. As a result, I got sick every other week or so. To mitigate colds and flus, I recommend packing some aspirin and/or over-the-counter allergy pills. While you can obtain both in the Philippines, it's best to be prepared; you don't want to have to stumble all the way to the mall with a throbbing headache and a temperature of 104, then have to sit and watch a pharmacist laboriously dole out the pills for you (you can't buy them over-the-counter for some reason).

Water quality tends to vary depending on where you are. While the travel clinic I went to urged me to avoid using Philippine tap water for anything—including brushing my teeth—the tap water at my Davao and Manila apartments never gave me any issues. On the other hand, when I was waiting in the Davao airport, I watched all of the water in the building—not just sinks and water foundations, but even *toilet water*—turn an incredibly gross shade of brown. To be on the safe side, stock bottled water in your fridge and boil water whenever you need to cook. Additionally, when you have guests over, serve them bottled water; it's considered poor etiquette to offer tap water.

To avoid food poisoning, don't eat at malls. Not only is mall food overpriced and inferior to freestanding restaurants, quality control is lacking. The only time I got diarrhea in the Philippines was when I ate at an "American-style" diner in Davao that served me a gigantic, awful-tasting burger prepared by a cook that probably forgot to wash his hands. If you want to eat at a restaurant, pop your head in and look around; if it appears clean, you're good to go. Additionally, when ordering drinks at a Philippine restaurant, be sure to ask for some ice, since many places skimp on refrigeration to save money. When shopping at grocery stores, be on guard as well; I once saw a roach darting out of the meat section of a supermarket.

Finally, watch out for sunburns and sun poisoning, particularly if you're fair-skinned. My advice is to wear pants at all times unless you're at the beach, swimming or doing something that requires shorts or swimming trunks. Similarly, you should avoid flip-flops and other open-toed shoes except during periods where you need them; flip-flops and cargo shorts are the uniform of the sex tourist. Wear a hat if possible and slather any exposed skin with sunscreen.

The Philippines on a Budget

Given how cheap the Philippines already is, you won't have to work too hard to get the maximum value out of your trip. If you rent an apartment, cook at home, and avoid overpriced mall eateries, you can live in a nice part of whatever city you want to visit for less than $1,500 a month.

As I mentioned already, you'll want to rent an apartment not only because it's cheaper than a hotel, it'll make it *much* easier for you to bang girls. Given the Philippines' patina of sexual conservatism, no Filipina will sleep with you if doing so will make her feel like a slut afterwards. By renting an apartment, you'll at least be putting on the *appearance* of settling down in the country.

After your flight and your lodging, most costs you'll run into are small and manageable. You could even make it rain some nights without breaking the bank. Here are some sample costs:

- Dinner at a good restaurant: $8
- Local beer at douchey club: $2
- Local beer at dive bar: $1.50

- Cover charge at douchey club: $5
- Short taxi ride: $3
- Can of tuna paella from supermarket: $0.65
- Cup of coffee from decent café: $4

Manila is by far the most expensive city in the Philippines, but even there, you'd be hard-pressed to burn more than $1,500 a month, unless you insist on getting toasted every night at Makati's most expensive clubs. Smaller, less touristy cities are even cheaper: for example, you can get by on $800-1,000 a month in Davao.

Now that you have all the info you need about living in the Philippines without getting ripped off or gang-banged in a dark alley, let's talk about the girls.

II

THE GIRLS

While I had a vague impression of what Filipino girls were like before I visited, I was almost completely unprepared for what I would encounter. Western men like to stereotype Filipinas as being "little brown fucking machines," and while you'll encounter plenty of slutty girls in the Philippines, the sheer number of chaste, honest girls will blow you away.

A reader of mine I met in Davao characterized Filipinas as either "virgins" or "sluts," with little to no middle ground, and I have to say that I agree. Whether your goal is to plow your way through dozens of girls or find a wife and mother of your children, the Philippines has something to offer you. I didn't subtitle this book "How to Make Love with Filipino Girls" for nothing.

Body and Appearance

Filipinas have a surprisingly wide spectrum of body types, probably reflective of the country's nature as the melting pot of Asia. However, you can generalize what Filipinas look like based on their racial characteristics. All Filipinas fall along a racial spectrum, with whiter/European girls at one end and browner/Asian girls at the other, both having divergent body types.

Browner, more Asian Filipinas tend to have more voluptuous body types, with big tits and bubble butts. Given that Asian girls are stereotyped as being flat chested and skinny, I was surprised at just how much junk some pinays have in their trunks. All Filipinas tend to be on the petite side—you'd be hard-pressed to find one over 5'3" who *isn't* a tranny—but the browner girls are shorter on average than the whiter girls are, with most topping out around the 5'0" range. While many of these girls are a bit chubby, they're not even *close* to the planetoid levels of obesity you'll see in the U.S.

The one issue with these girls is that they tend to be butterfaces. You'll often be walking through a mall or down a sidewalk checking out a girl with a firm, juicy, round ass, only to recoil a little when you see her face. Brown Filipinas tend to have large, wide noses, weird cheeks, and lips that seem oversized for their faces. It's in part because of this that some upper class Filipinos will look down on foreigners who date or marry more Asian-looking Filipinas.

Given the importance that Philippine culture places on whiteness, girls who are more Asian looking tend to be insecure about their looks. It's common for Filipinas with large boobs or butts to try to hide them when they're in public. Because of this, picking up and banging brown Filipinas is like shooting fish in a barrel... dead fish. Brown pinays are so accustomed to being ignored that if they get the slightest amount of attention from a foreigner, they'll treat him like a god.

More European-looking Filipinas are closer to what you'd expect from Asian girls: thin, petite bodies, dark hair and pale skin. While they lack the boobs and butts of their lower-class counterparts, they make up for it with prettier faces. Virtually all of the Philippines' most famous celebrities (actors, musicians etc.) have at least some European ancestry, and Chinese ancestry is more common among the upper class (a third of all Filipinos are at least part Chinese). Because white skin and European features are considered so desirable in the Philippines, whiter Filipinas are in high demand among men, so if you go after them, you'll also be competing with Filipino guys.

In general, the wealthier a city, the more likely that its womenfolk will tend towards the white end of the spectrum. For example, in Manila, Makati is the place you want to go if you want to meet European-looking Filipinas. As you get further into the provinces, the girls will become browner and more Asian. I only saw a handful of European-looking girls in Davao, and I didn't get the chance to bang any while I was there.

It's worth noting that many Filipinas are unable to maintain their body weight as they get older. Due to the country's fattening cuisine as well as the increasing prevalence of heart-attack-on-a-plate restaurant chains like KFC and Kenny Rogers' Roasters, many Filipinas start blimping up when they hit their thirties. Fortunately, given how big the Philippines' population is—and Filipinos' predilection for procreating like meth-addled rats—there's little reason for you to bother with girls over thirty, even if you yourself are in your thirties or older.

Overall, I'd say that Filipinas tend to hover in the 5-7 range of female beauty. You'll see plenty of cute or mediocre girls on an average day, but few if any truly stunning beauties. The only truly unfuckable girls will either be beggars or old ladies. As a result, if you go out on an average night, 80 to 90 percent of the girls you meet will be bangable.

The main problem with Filipinas is having to choose between the brown girls and the white girls. Brown girls are much easier to pick up, nail and please, but their butterfaces can wear on you after a while. While white girls have cuter faces, their bodies are less curvy and they also have bigger egos due to the hordes of thirsty Filipino guys hitting on them. If you're looking for the complete package in the Philippines, you're not likely to get it.

The average Filipina's style is best described as "demure yet sexy." During the day, they stick to T-shirts, sleeveless shirts, jeans, skirts with leggings, sandals and sneakers. They'll also put on makeup to look good, even if they're just going grocery shopping. Even poorer Filipinas dress with more dignity than your average white trust-fund hipster back home does. When they show skin, it's not in an attempt to look slutty, but purely so they don't sweat to death in the sun. You'll also notice many girls using umbrellas in the sunshine so they don't get tanned or sunburned. While their appearances leave a lot to the imagination, the average Filipina carries herself with a feminine energy that makes her look sexy even if she's not particularly dressed up.

At the beach, you can distinguish more chaste girls from sluts by their choice of swimwear. Girls that are more conservative will wear one-piece bathing suits that cover up their torsos, while sluts wear bikinis. Girls who wear bikinis have usually lived abroad in the West, where they also absorbed Western sexual mores. At night, girls wear high heels and dresses, and while they're sluttier-looking—and just plain sluttier—than the norm (chaste Filipinas don't go to bars or clubs alone), they have a level of class that is almost absent in the West these days. The average Filipina's style suggests a reserved girl who has a dirty side that she's just dying to indulge with the right man.

Additionally, when you're out at the bars and clubs, you'll often feel so overwhelmed with choice when it comes to girls that you'll never be truly satisfied. So many times when I was barhopping in Manila, I'd be talking to one cute girl only for a cuter girl to start checking me out. In the Philippines, you'll never be able to shake the feeling that you could be doing better than the girl or girls you're banging at the moment.

In general, the Philippines is not a place you want to go if you want to be surrounded with mind-blowing female beauty. While you'll be hard-up when it comes to girls you *wouldn't* want to sleep with, nothing about Filipinas justifies having high standards for their looks. What sells the Philippines as a poosy paradise is how easy the girls are to get into bed and how sweet they treat you. Besides, if you get bored of one girl, you can always sleep around on her.

Personality

What really made me fall in love with the Philippines was the way that the girls treated me. On average, Filipinas are so pleasant, girly and nurturing that it's impossible to not have a good time with one. Even if a girl wasn't as attractive as I would have liked, her femininity and eagerness to please kept me around, at least for a little bit.

To begin with, virtually all Filipinas you'll meet are sweet to the point of being downright treacly. Even girls who don't want to sleep with you will be so nice about rejecting you that you won't even feel bad. Because Filipinas haven't been conditioned to hate and fear men in the same way that American girls have, they won't brutally shoot you down just for kicks. Filipino girls don't treat men like clowns that are there to entertain them, so they won't reject you just for making a bad joke or insult you for the sake of insulting you.

Filipinas are also incredibly nurturing. A Filipina's highest goal in life is to find a man whom she can serve and care for. If you get into a relationship with a girl, don't be surprised if she starts offering to cook for you, clean your apartment and do other nice things to make you happy. For example, when I mentioned to one of my Davao girlfriends that I was sick, she insisted that I let her run to the pharmacy for some medicine and stay the night to make sure I was all right. Even sluttier, more Westernized girls have some of these nurturing qualities. The average Filipina's desire to satisfy her man makes her a great mother. More than once when I was over in the Philippines, I kept thinking to myself, "Y'know, if I accidentally got this girl pregnant, it wouldn't be so bad."

Next, Filipinas are incredibly feminine. Even though their daily dress is more functional than flashy, they always try to look attractive for men by wearing makeup and earrings. For example, virtually all cashiers you'll come across wear lipstick. I became so inured to the femininity of Filipinas that when I ran across an Australian girl waddling around the immigration office in Davao, I was almost taken aback. She was twenty pounds overweight, had buck teeth, and was seething with resentment and sexual frustration. It's clear that wherever she was from, she was used to men kissing her ass just for being female, but in a land where girls are feminine and take care of themselves, she'd been relegated to freak show status.

As a corollary to this, Filipinas become insecure when they don't look 100 percent their best. Even if she's just coming over to your place to watch a movie, she'll be done up as if she's going clubbing. No matter how long you've been together, she'll always remain self-conscious of her appearance and want to look as hot as possible.

Because Filipinos are generally fluent in English and follow American TV and movies, the cultural barrier between the girls and you is a lot lower than it ordinarily would be. While Filipinas have their own cultural quirks, you can have a conversation with one and she'll be able to understand your jokes and pop culture references. This makes wooing girls with your verbal acuity a lot easier than in other foreign countries.

While Filipinas take education seriously, they don't allow their schooling to get in the way of their relationships.

Even girls studying to be lawyers or computer engineers are just as feminine and charming as other Filipinas. In fact, living in the Philippines forced me to reevaluate my belief that college education ruins girls' personalities and makes them unsuitable to be wives and mothers. While Filipinas aspire to learn and to get good jobs, they don't place their careers ahead of their desire to get married and have children. To Filipinas, jobs are something you do to get money and nothing more.

Next, Filipinas cause less drama than American girls. While pinays tend to get jealous and clingy, they won't start fights without a good reason, nor will they hold minor slights against you. While I did get into a huge fight with one girl in Davao, it was because *I* was being an asshole and I deserved it. If you've been laboring under the assumption that all relationships involve violent arguments and constant bickering, you'll find Filipinas to be pleasantly tranquil.

While Filipinas try to play games with men they don't know well, once you've seen her a couple times, she'll drop the act. When you're dating a Filipina, she'll wear her heart on her sleeve and make it clear that she cares about you. Filipinas in more liberal cities like Manila tend to play more games and are harder to crack, but if you're in a more conservative city like Davao, don't be surprised if you have girls telling you that they love you after a few weeks. It's entirely possible that their weak-ass game playing works on chump Filipino dudes, but unless you're a basement-dwelling virgin, you'll be able to tell a Filipina's next move from miles away.

While many Filipinas tend to sleep around—particularly in the more tourist-heavy cities—you'll also encounter a lot of girls who want to settle down with one man. As a result, once you've gotten a girl into bed, you can make her your girlfriend almost immediately afterwards. This is best done in cities that are more conservative; given the Filipino attitude of living in the moment, girls in Manila and similar places tend to hop from guy to guy, never mind that they all claim they're "sick" of players or whatever.

Filipinas are absolute demons in the sack. While their Catholic beliefs tend to make them outwardly reserved, once you've turned a girl on, she'll fuck you until you can't take it anymore. More chaste girls will need to be trained up, but after a few dates, you'll be able to mold her into the perfect slut. Just remember that virtually all Filipinas have ludicrously tight pussies, and browner girls tend to have shorter pussies as well. If you're average or above average in size, you're not going to be able to fully penetrate a good portion of the girls you bang. Additionally, Filipinas' vice-grip pussies can initially make having sex with you painful for them, particularly if they're virgins. For this reason, I recommend having a bottle of K-Y or Astroglide handy so you can ease your battering ram into her iron gates of life.

Finally, Filipinas have strong family values. It's common to see girls holding hands with their mothers at the mall and treating each other affectionately. To a Filipina, her family is the most important thing in her life, and she remains close with not only her parents and siblings, but her extended family as well. It's because of these close family ties that Filipinas make such great wives and mothers; indeed, when you visit, you'll often find yourself wondering why you *shouldn't* get married and create your own brood of halfie kids.

The only real downside of the Filipina personality is how reserved they are in public. Because of the country's Catholic-influenced culture, Filipinas will not be super-affectionate with you when you're out, nor do they dress in a way that will make your hard-on strain against your jeans. In public, Filipinas behave in a very wholesome fashion, and you won't truly see them at their best until you're alone with one.

Another possible downside (or upside, depending on your perspective) to Filipinas is their lack of future time orientation. As I've mentioned before, Filipinos very much live in the moment and usually don't think their actions through. This makes it easy as cake to get a Filipina into bed—simply make her feel good and continually move the seduction forward—but can also lead to other problems down the road. For example, take this account from Roosh V Forum member iknowexactly, who discussed how he asked a Filipina if she wanted to have a baby and she said yes right away; i.e., she wanted to have a baby *right at that moment.*[3]

It's their public demureness and their unattractive faces that knock the Philippines out of the highest echelon of poosy paradise. Depending on your preferences in girls, you may find Filipinas' butterfaces and Catholic hang-ups too much to deal with. In particular, the lack of truly hot girls may be a deal-breaker, particularly if you have excellent game. Despite all this, given how wonderful Filipino girls are to be around, it's impossible to have a bad time when you're visiting.

Types of Filipino Girls

There are five types of girls you'll encounter in the Philippines: hookers, college students, twentysomething professionals, single moms, and cougars.

It's worth mentioning hookers for the simple reason that it's impossible to avoid them in places like Manila. Hookers are distinguished primarily by the fact that they'll come on to *you:* normal Filipinas are too shy to approach men, particularly foreign men, on their own. While I can't stop you from paying for sex, I don't do it myself and this book is not aimed at whoremongers. It's possible to "shore" hookers (get them to sleep with you for free because they're genuinely attracted to you), but you're selling yourself short by concentrating on girls who do pay-for-play for a living.

In general, avoid hookers and if they try to force themselves on you, be polite but firm in telling them you're not interested.

College students will be your bread and butter in the Philippines, particularly if you concentrate on online game. They tend to be between the ages of 18 and 24, have grown up absorbing American pop culture, are intensely curious about foreigners and foreign men in particular, are inexperienced when it comes to playing games, and are more easily impressed. Additionally, since many of them are away from home for the first time, they're looking to get naughty away from the prying eyes of their families. While they can be flaky at times, there's so many of them—thanks to the Philippines' exploding birth rate—that you can instantly line up another girl if one of them pisses you off.

If you're worried about college girls blowing you off because you're too old, don't. In fact, many Filipinas actually prefer older men (thirties and up) because they tend to be more mature and are more established in their careers. In fact, I was probably at a bit of a disadvantage in the Philippines because I was only 26 when I visited. While you may encounter some problems the older you are, you won't encounter enough to matter.

The ideal way to meet college girls is online via FilipinoCupid, a dating site that specializes in matching Filipino girls with foreign men. Another good method is through day game at malls. You may also be able to find them at bars, particularly in larger cities like Manila, but given these girls' limited budgets, they don't tend to party as often as other Filipinas.

The one problem with college students (as well as more working-class girls you may encounter in the same age bracket) is that they're so busy much of the time that they can't hang out too often. Filipinas take college seriously, so they're unlikely to choose some random guy over their studies, at least before you get the bang. Similarly, with girls who work as cashiers or similar jobs, they often have to work twelve hours a day, six days a week due to the Philippines' lax labor laws. Fortunately, even in more conservative cities, it shouldn't take you more than two or three dates to get the lay.

Next up is the twentysomething professional. These girls are more common in wealthier areas such as Makati or Quezon City, hanging out in bars and clubs. They tend to be 25 to 29, work reasonably good jobs (lawyers, engineers etc.), and often have traveled abroad, to the U.S. or other Western countries. They've also usually absorbed the looser sexual mores of the countries they've gone to. While these girls won't be as wowed by your foreign status as college girls, they're still easy to connect with and their increased sluttiness makes picking them up easy as pie. Additionally, since many Filipinas marry or at least have children in their teens or early twenties, these girls tend to be overlooked by men.

Girls in this age bracket tend to be outwardly searching for a husband or long-term boyfriend. Their dating profiles on FilipinoCupid are often peppered with statements like "NO PLAYERS!" and "I'm tired of boys who play games." Don't buy any of it: these girls are no harder to bang than any other type of Filipina. In fact, if you're in a liberal city like Manila, you should assume that other men are also railing the Filipinas you bang. Given the city's libertine atmosphere and the average Filipino's lack of forethought, few of these girls are probably even aware of what they're doing.

Next, let's talk about single moms. They tend to be between the ages of 18 and 29 and overlap with college girls, working-class girls and professionals. Single moms are (obviously) distinguished by the little brat(s) they have in tow. These girls are super-desperate to find a foreign man on whom they can pawn off their kid; you'll usually find them online or in malls during the day. They flake far less than other types of girls and are more outwardly agreeable, but are more apt to play games in an attempt to ensnare you in a relationship. Because most Filipinas retain close bonds with their extended families, they can freely leave their kid with a relative so they can go cavorting around the city with you.

There is no reason for you to bother with single moms. None whatsoever. It sucks that whoever knocked 'em up decided to run and leave 'em with the bill, but it's not your duty to care for some broad's cuckoo's egg. Additionally, Filipinas who've had kids look gross with their clothes off: stretch marks, chewed-up nipples, and excess poundage galore. Filipinas themselves are acutely aware that having a kid makes them damaged goods, which is why they'll try to downplay being single moms or outright lie about it. For example, I was messaging one girl and after getting her number, she conveniently decides to tell me that she's pregnant. I blocked her straight away. Don't bang single moms. There are so many fish in the Filipina sea that you can find one who *hasn't* gotten pregnant with zero effort.

Finally, we have cougars. These girls tend to be 30 and up and usually overlap with the professional set (Filipinas who are single moms at that age have usually given up on romance). Imagine twentysomething professionals with a side of horniness and an extra helping of crazy. Because of the Philippines' high birth rate—and the resultant huge population of young people—cougars are all but invisible and are desperate for dick as a result. You'll usually find them at bars and occasionally at clubs. Cherry Blossoms, another dating site that helps Filipinas connect with foreign men, also has a lot of cougars.

Much like with single moms, there's no real reason to bother with cougars, since there are more than enough younger, cuter girls to sate your lusts. Having said that, some of these girls can surprise you. While Filipinas don't age as well as other types of Asian girls, you can still find some lookers in the 30 and up age bracket. If you see a cougar you're attracted to, just go for it.

While transsexuals are almost as common in the Philippines as they are in Thailand, they're easy to avoid. Trannies are considerably taller than the average woman is and are more aggressive as well due to their hormonal issues. Additionally, Mark Zolo shared a tip with me that rang true: Filipino trannies will often try to come on to you by telling you that they're on their period, but they can go down on you and you can come on their tits. Don't fall for it. Unless you spend a lot of time in sleazy go-go bars and other sex tourist-infested parts of the Philippines, you're unlikely to run into trannies.

Summary

After three months in the Philippines, I'd say that the stereotype of Filipinas being easy is true. Even good girls will go horizontal for you after only a couple of dates, though this is more due to the country's "if it feels good, do it" mentality than anything else. Stick to college girls and professionals and the only nights you *won't* be able to get laid are the nights that you don't *want* to get laid.

If you're looking for a long-term girlfriend or a wife, the Philippines is also a great place to go. If you stick to cities that are more conservative and choose the right girls, you can find one who will be loyal to you and treat you like a king. Filipinas' easygoing nature and feminine wiles make dating and banging them a sublime experience.

III

GAME

If you're an American or from another Western country, I've got news that will have you jumping for joy: your existing game will work on Filipino girls with only a few tweaks. While it'd be an exaggeration to say that the only game you need in the Philippines is showing up, it wouldn't be too far from the truth. Even if you're not as experienced with American/Western girls as you would like, you can easily crack the Filipina code in just a few days provided you actually get out of the house and talk to girls.

The ideal type of game to use in the Philippines is what author Roosh V describes in *Bang Poland* as "confident nice guy game." Essentially, have a backbone, but also let your romantic side show. Filipinas are ostensibly looking for men who can protect and provide for them: husband material. If you can keep them under your thumb while letting your softer, "beta" side out at the same time, you will absolutely *kill it* with Filipinas.

Before I discuss how to pick up Filipino girls though, I'll tell you what kinds of men they go for. Put simply, Filipinas love foreigners, white men most of all, and white American men in particular. Since whiter/more European-looking Filipinos have higher social status, Filipinas aspire to be white and almost all of them dream of marrying a white guy. To see this in action for yourself, I recommend checking out the Philippine edition of *Cosmopolitan*. Not only is the content more nakedly sexual than the American version of the magazine, the bulk of the male models in the Philippine *Cosmo* are Caucasian.

For further confirmation of how much Filipinas are into white men, you can try a little experiment. Open up an account on FilipinoCupid or a similar site that helps Filipinas meet foreign men. Post a decent picture of yourself (it doesn't have to be super nice, it just has to clearly show that you're white and don't have open running sores on your face) and type something random for your profile description. Then sit back and watch your inbox blow up. When I signed up for FilipinoCupid, I had to disable email notifications almost immediately because I was getting dozens of emails an hour from Filipinas messaging me, liking my profile or even just looking at it. Most of the time, they didn't even read what I wrote: the fact that I was white and American was enough for them.

In general, you'll need to adjust your game somewhat depending on what part of the country you're in.

In a tourist-heavy joint like Manila with progressive sexual mores, you'll have to be a bit cockier with girls to get them interested (though not even *half* as cocky as you need to be with American girls). The rarer foreigners are in your city, the more you can indulge your beta side; in fact, girls will expect it. Just don't let them walk all over you. Similarly, you'll need to be cockier with whiter-looking Filipinas and more romantic with Asian-looking ones.

If you're a white guy and you walk into a bar or club that's not frequented by foreigners, all eyes will be on you. Bartenders will give you preferential service (particularly if you tip; always tip), girls will check you out, and everyone will want to be your friend. It's mind-blowing to walk into a venue and be the coolest guy there without having to do anything. It's because of this—and because it was so easy to pull girls—that I actually *enjoyed* the kinds of douchey club and lounge scenes that I despise back home.

One contributing factor to your success with Filipinas will be the horrendous game most Filipino guys have. Even discounting your advantage as a foreigner, Filipinos are total chodes when it comes to girls; their game consists of hovering around girls and offering to buy them drinks. They're also less willing to approach: the only time I ever saw Filipino guys approaching girls was bum rushing them on the dance floor. Most Filipinos' bangs come from running in the same social circles as the girls they nail. You'll have tougher competition in higher-end clubs and/or when you're dealing with more European-looking girls, but even then, you can spit standard American game and have a good chance of coming out on top.

Swooping girls in a bar or club is an absolute cinch. Given the eighties/early nineties vibe of Philippine culture, Filipinas will still be impressed that you have the balls to actually go up and talk to them. To test which girls are receptive to your approach, scan your eyeballs around and look for one you like, and then make eye contact. If she returns your eye contact for a few seconds, head on over and talk to her. This won't guarantee that she'll be sucking your dick later that night, but it shows she's at least open to the idea. If you're good at dancing, you'll be able to use this to great effect, as most Filipinos are into dancing at clubs and karaoke bars.

Also, don't worry about ratios. In American bars and clubs, an excessive ratio of cocks to clams will pretty much kill your chances of getting laid because all the guys will descend on the few attractive girls, inflating their egos to ludicrous degrees. However, in a Philippine bar or club, *you* are a celebrity. Do you think Brad Pitt, Chief Keef or any other famous figure worries about club ratios? Of course not: they're so much higher in status than all the other dudes that it doesn't matter.

While the best nights to go out in the Philippines are Thursdays, Fridays and Saturdays, there's really no reason not to go out on other nights unless you have something more important going on. Even on slow nights in Manila, you're assured of getting a number—if not an outright bang—provided you get out of the house and approach. While it sounds like I'm putting pressure on you, don't worry about it; it's nearly impossible to go wrong in the Philippines.

If you're not white, don't worry; Filipinas are by far the least bigoted and most xenophilic people in Asia. Black guys in particular can slay ass left and right; while in Davao, I linked up with a black reader of mine who was getting laid more than me. I can't speak for other races, but I don't see why they'd run into any issues. In fact, the only way I can think you'd be at a *huge* disadvantage in the Philippines is if you're Filipino yourself (born and raised abroad) or look Filipino, since you won't have exoticness working in your favor.

The best way to compare the ease of getting laid for white guys versus black guys (and presumably other ethnicities) in the Philippines is like comparing a man who has $20 billion versus one who has $15 billion. Sure, the guy with $20 billion has more money than you, but you each have more money than either of you will be able to spend. You'll be too busy splitting Filipina pussies open like pieces of wood to worry about whether someone else is getting *slightly* more ass.

Essentially, night game in the Philippines works like it did in the U.S. circa 1999. Approach girls, entertain them and make them laugh with your conversation, maybe buy them a drink, then take them back to your lair for a good, hard pounding. Chances are if you read my blog, you already know how to do all this. If you want some tips, I recommend checking out Roosh's book *Bang:* it'll show you how to pick up girls at night consistently and easily. If you can pull ass in American/Western bars and clubs, picking up Filipinas is the equivalent of playing *Metal Gear Solid* on the easiest difficulty setting, where you're given a machine gun with infinite ammo.

Despite this, night game isn't even close to being the best way to get laid in the Philippines, particularly in smaller cities with quieter nightlife scenes. While you're a fool if you don't check out nightlife spots in Manila and larger cities, the bulk of your bangs are going to come from online and day game.

Online Game

Online game is where I absolutely killed it with Filipinas: the largest share of my bangs in the Philippines was from girls I met via the Internet. Most Filipinas have access to the Internet, at their jobs, schools, at home or via their cell phones, and many of them use online dating sites to connect with foreign men. Unlike Western girls, who use online dating sites purely to attention whore, Filipinas actually *want* to meet men.

The best site to use by far is FilipinoCupid. A wide variety of girls use the site, from sluts looking to get rammed with big white cocks to ladies looking for a foreign husband. As I mentioned in the previous section, your value as a foreigner is so high on FilipinoCupid that you'll be inundated with messages and notifications the minute you put up a profile picture. It doesn't matter where you say you are or what you write in your profile: you'll have tons of girls telling you how "handsome" you are, checking out your picture, or trying to suck up to you.

In fact, it wasn't until I started dating Filipinas that I truly understood what it was like to be an attractive woman. American and Western girls are inundated with attention everywhere they go, just for being female: they get special privileges in their daily lives, men trip over themselves to help them out, and their online dating profiles are stuffed to the brim with messages from interchangeable chumps trying to get their attention. In the Philippines, *I* was in the same boat, constantly getting attention from girls I wasn't interested in, who didn't care about my personality or who I really was, who just saw me as a cool white guy who might put a ring on it.

If you want to get started with FilipinoCupid, you can sign up for a free account. A free membership will let you set up your profile and search for girls, though you'll need to upgrade to a paid account if you want to actually message them (as well as read messages they send you); it's absolutely worth the money.

You don't have to put too much thought into designing your profile, but here are some pointers. Fill out all the information about yourself honestly (you don't need to fudge the facts about your age or height) and write a brief description of yourself that accentuates your positive attributes. For example, if you're a writer, mention that you're a writer. Don't brag about being rich or having money, because you'll attract gold-diggers and scammers. Also, talk about the kind of girl you're looking for, writing it in such a fashion that you don't disqualify any girls who check out your profile. Don't mention anything about yourself that puts you in a negative light. For example, don't say that you do drugs (even if you do).

After drafting your profile, you'll want to rewrite it in a fashion that makes you look mysterious and enigmatic. The goal is to give out enough information to get girls interested in you and want to learn more. For example, in my profile, I mentioned that I was an "author," but that "I won't tell you the names of the books I've written just yet." Think of yourself as a fisherman and the girls you're messaging as fish. You want to throw out enough bait to reel them in; too much bait and they'll just gobble it down and swim away. If you want more specific pointers, I recommend checking out Nicholas Jack's book *Elite Online*

Dating, which I used to help design my FilipinoCupid profile.

When it comes to picture selection, choose photos that make you look as good as possible. Pictures of you doing exciting things (hiking, waterskiing, playing guitar) or pics of you with your friends will both work. You should avoid using pictures of you kissing or otherwise being intimate with other girls; while these pics help attract attention from Western girls, Filipinas will assume you're a dreaded "player."

After you've set up your profile, it's time to start messaging girls. The *very first message* you send to a girl should be something along these lines:

> *Hi [GIRL'S NAME HERE], I'm moving to Davao in two weeks… how are you doing?*

Your first message to the girl should be telling her that you're going to be in her city soon or that you're already there. Why? Because there are a lot of guys on FilipinoCupid who hit girls up solely because they're looking for cam sex. By telling her that you're going to be in her city (or are already there), you reassure her that you're not some creep. Don't bother personalizing your initial message beyond using her name, because you'll be messaging so many girls—and the girls themselves will be so interchangeable—that you'll quickly go insane.

When it comes to girls who message you, feel free to reply with something similar if you're interested in them. Hotter girls will not message you but will simply view your profile, sometimes more than once. To get them hooked, send them a joking message along the lines of, "Hey, don't just come over to my profile without saying hi!"

Her response to your message will determine what you do next. If a girl is interested in you, she'll make it obvious with her reply. If she's not interested, she'll say something along the lines of "Oh, well, enjoy your stay!" She may also tell you that she no longer lives in the city in question. Additionally, this is where you'll get scammers trying to get you to send them money by barraging you with nonstop sob stories. I've had Filipinas whine to me about their college tuition, their textbooks, the cost of raising their kids, and even one girl who told me she had a "funeral problem."

If a Filipina ever starts complaining about her life or trying to wheedle cash out of you at *any* point in the relationship, next her. You're not her personal ATM. Honest Filipinas deal with their problems with dignity and are too proud to ask for handouts from foreigners. For example, I once tried to give a girl I met in Davao money for a taxi and she flatly refused. Filipinas who constantly drone on about their money issues and personal problems view relationships as purely transactional and are looking to bilk you for all you're worth. If they don't like your attitude, they can go fleece someone else.

    Back to the messaging. If the girl is interested in you and she's not trying to get money out of you, it's time to escalate things. My guiding principle when it comes to online dating is to *get the interaction into the real world as soon as possible.* In the case of Filipinas, you want to get their phone numbers so you can start texting them. The last thing you want is to get sucked into messaging back and forth on FilipinoCupid all day.

    Therefore, your next message should tell the girl that you want to meet her for coffee (if you're in a more liberal area like Manila, you can tell her you want to grab a drink instead) and you don't want to waste time on FilipinoCupid, then ask for her number. Nine times out of ten, the girls will give it up. If she doesn't give you her number straightaway, you may have to exchange a few more messages, but she'll eventually comply. After you've gotten her number, tell her that you'll text her when you get to her city (or you'll text her soon, if you're already in her city), and you're off to the races.

    Nicholas Jack/20Nation recommends webcamming with a girl as an intermediate step between messaging her and meeting her in the real world, particularly if you haven't arrived in the Philippines yet.[4] According to him, talking to a girl over Skype or a similar program reduces the likelihood that she'll flake when it comes to the date, because she has an idea of what you're like in real life. I never tried webcamming myself, but it's worth a shot. In my experience, getting Filipinas to go out on dates is so easy that flakiness is almost a non-factor: as soon as one girl drops off, another one shows up.

Finally, don't get hung up on any particular girl. You don't know what someone is like until you've met them in person, and your dream Filipina could be an absolute nightmare in the flesh. Message as many girls as you can and get as many numbers as you can so you can start lining up dates when you arrive. Ideally, you want at least one girl for each night of the week, and possibly more if you don't mind going out with multiple girls in a day. If you don't have at least one date lined up by the time you arrive in the country, you're wasting your time and money.

How early should you start pipelining (messaging) girls via online dating? The consensus is that for more conservative cities, you need to start pipelining earlier in order to get past the girls' demure personalities. Personally, I began pipelining girls via FilipinoCupid *two weeks* before I arrived in Davao and *one week* before I arrived in Manila. Pipelining girls more than a month before your trip is likely a waste given Filipinas' short attention spans and lack of future time orientation.

Before I go, it's worth mentioning two other online dating sites you can use for meeting Filipinas: Cherry Blossoms and Date in Asia. Cherry Blossoms is a paid service like FilipinoCupid, the main differences being that it includes women from all over Asia (not just the Philippines) and the girls on it tend to be 30 and up. While I didn't use it while I was in the Philippines, I ran some experiments using it when I went to research this book: the game tactics that will work for FilipinoCupid will work for Cherry Blossoms.

Date in Asia is a complete waste of time. It's the only completely free online dating site in this section, but you get what you pay for: tons of scammers, fake profiles and trannies. While I had an account on the site, I wasn't able to get any bangs from it. Don't bother with it. Additionally, while it's possible to use Tinder, OkCupid and other Western-focused dating sites in the Philippines, I personally didn't bother because of the wealth of pussy I was able to find on FilipinoCupid.

Day Game

Day game in the Philippines will be your other primary method of getting laid. Indeed, meeting Filipinas during the day is so easy that I almost feel bad for the girls; they have no idea what hit them. Like with day game back in the West, you'll want to brush up on the basics before you head to the Philippines, so I recommend Roosh's *Day Bang* for general information on how to talk to girls during the day.

The easiest place to meet Filipino girls during the day is at the mall. As I've mentioned already, Filipinos love malls. Mall culture in the Philippines is similar to mall culture in the U.S. circa the mid-90's: teenagers go there to hang out, families go there to have fun together, and girls go there to window-shop. Not only that, malls' air conditioning provides a welcome respite from the Philippines' constant heat and humidity, and they're also a safe place to hang out (virtually all malls have armed guards and metal detectors to deter bad guys).

So you know where to go to meet girls, but what do you say to them? The answer: you barely need to say anything at all. This day game tip I learned from Mark Zolo and Nicholas Jack is how you reel the girls in.[5]

First, go to the store and get yourself a notebook and some pens, if you don't have them already. Tear out a sheet of paper, and then tear *that* into 10-12 smaller pieces. On each piece, write your first name (in all capital letters), your Philippine phone number, and a little cutesy doodle (a heart with an arrow through it works well). Don't make the notes too elaborate; you want them to look like you wrote them in a hurry. They should be legible but not *too* fancy. When you're done, stuff them in your pants pocket.

When you're ready to go out and talk to girls, head to the bathroom and spruce yourself up a bit. Take a shower, shave, brush your teeth, wear a nice shirt; again, the idea is to look your best without coming off as try-hard. (You should be doing this anyway.)

When you get to the mall (or wherever you're planning to meet girls), look around for single girls that you're attracted to. When you spot one you want to bang, coolly walk up to her, say hi, and give her one of the notes while saying, "This is for you." Smile a bit, but don't overdo it or you'll look like a clown. If you can, try to get her name, but don't worry too much if you don't. Then turn around and walk away, maybe waving back to the girl as you're heading off. Repeat until you've handed out all your notes.

When I used this day game method, anywhere from *60 to 70 percent* of Filipinas I gave my number to would text me back within hours.

Why is this method so effective? One, because it's discreet. Even in lustful cities like Manila, Filipinas don't want to be seen as sluts, which they might if they're seen talking to a foreigner they don't know for too long. By handing her a note, you're both directly approaching her (showing her you're a man of confidence), yet there's no pressure on her and no one to potentially witness the prelude to the sinful acts she wants to engage in.

Secondly, this method allows you to get around any potential language barriers. Filipinas are generally unaccustomed to men approaching them during the day, and in less cosmopolitan cities like Davao, they can get so flustered and bashful that their English goes straight out the window. This method eliminates the need for you to woo her with any conversation.

Finally, handing a girl a note puts her in the driver's seat. By giving her a note and walking away, you're signifying that while you're interested in her, you have things to do and can't putz around all day window-shopping with her. She's put in the position of having to chase *you*. If she texts you back, you already know she likes you, reducing the likelihood of flaking.

This method is really all the day game you need.

Texting and Calling

99.9 percent of your phone communications with Filipinas will be via text, mainly because texting is incredibly cheap in the Philippines. Filipinos have taken to texting like flies to coprophagia: if you text one, expect them to respond within five to ten minutes, and if *you* don't respond to their text within the same time span, they'll start blowing your phone up with messages asking if *you're* okay.

When it comes to Filipinas you haven't slept with, the guiding principle of texting is the same as messaging them on dating sites: *getting the interaction into the real world as soon as possible.* To this end, gear your initial texts with her towards setting up a date. There's not a lot of brainpower involved in texting a Filipina: flirt with her, tell her how you're doing when she asks, and just be a cool, normal guy. You don't need to memorize canned lines or pretend to be hard-ass so long as you don't overdo it with the sentimentality. You should be able to gauge how interested she is in you by how she responds; while it doesn't mean much if she uses smiley faces, no smilies at all is a red flag.

The ideal first date location in the Philippines is a coffee shop, usually a Starbucks since American brands are popular among Filipinos. If you're in a more liberal city like Manila, you can also substitute the coffee date with a drink date. Don't *ever* go on dinner dates, and don't ever accept a girl's idea for a first date. Either way, set a date, time and location and you're good to go.

Keep in mind that some girls will flake on you when date time rolls around, *or* they'll try to play games and change up the time or location. For example, I'd agreed to meet one girl at a Starbucks for a first date when she started texting me an hour before asking if we could move the date to a mall that was purportedly closer to her house... and miles away from me. It would have taken me nearly two hours to get to her suggested meeting spot, so I told her no and blocked her number.

If a girl starts playing games like that, next her without a second thought. If the girl really had a problem meeting me at that specific Starbucks, she would have told me before she agreed to do so. By changing up the location at the last minute, she was trying to see how well she could manipulate me. It's an obvious power play: if I had acceded to her demands, even if I had gotten the bang, she would have been dictating the terms of the relationship. Given the ocean of pussy that is the Philippines, there's no reason for you to waste time with an intransigent fish.

Also, note that due to Filipinos' flexible concept of timeliness, girls will tend to be either early or late to the date. Don't feel bad about showing up ten minutes late; if the girl likes you, she'll wait.

Going on Dates

From here on out, you can pretty much apply standard game in your quest to get Filipino girls in the sack. If you want an idea of how to handle yourself on a first date, check out Roosh's *Bang*. The basic idea is that you continue impressing the girl with your wit and wisdom while progressively touching her on the arms, eventually escalating to hugging and kissing.

The type of date you're on and where you are will determine how fast you'll be able to escalate. If you're at a bar in Manila, chances are high that you'll be balls deep in the girl before the night is up. Conversely, on a coffee date in Davao, you'll have to wait two, maybe three dates before the girl gets her clothes off. Follow your instincts as a man and you'll rarely go wrong.

One major red flag you should be on the lookout for on a first date is bad English, particularly if you're in a smaller city. Given that English is one of the Philippines' official languages and learning it is mandatory in schools, what does that say about girls who can barely speak it? Answer: they're dumb, lazy and talking to them will be as fun as a Novocain-free root canal on shrooms. For example, I once went on a date with a girl who was only capable of sending illiterate one-word texts, and most of our time together consisted of me pantomiming with my arms like a retard, praying that something would penetrate her thick skull. If a girl can barely understand English, next her.

If you need to go on a second date with a girl before she'll go horizontal, the ideal spot is the swimming pool at your place. (Your place *does* have a pool, right?) No red-blooded Filipina will be able to resist the allure of being able to go for a dip in a nice, refreshing swimming pool. Not only that, the increased amount of skin she'll be showing plus her need to change in and out of her bathing suit provides more opportunities for physical escalation. Alternately, you can take the girl to a private beach for a day of swimming, relaxing in the sun and building sand castles.

Note that sometimes Filipinas will ask if one of their friends can tag along with you on a date. This may *sound* like a game, but it's not. Filipinas will want to bring their friends along both for bragging rights *("Look at this cool white guy I'm dating!")* and safety reasons (since they may not fully trust you yet). Let her bring her friend. Like all girls, Filipinas' opinions are in part determined by their social group: if you make a good impression on her friends, you'll find it *much* easier to seal the deal with her.

If it seems like these sections are on the short side, it's because there really isn't a lot to say. Because Filipino girls haven't been trained to despise men in the same way that American girls have, you don't need particularly elaborate game tactics to bang them. Just carry yourself with confidence, don't give off a "player" vibe and you'll be good.

Managing Your Contacts

The only factor limiting how many Filipinas you nail is how much time you're willing to spend on pursuing them: messaging girls online, approaching them, and going on dates. If you're particularly motivated, you can bang *multiple girls a day* if you like. If your goal is pure numbers though, you'll need a system to keep yourself from mixing up girls.

I like Fisto's system of classifying girls by name, city and rating.[6] When putting the girls' numbers in your phone, assign them a 1–5 rating of how badly you want to bang them (ex: "Peaches Davao 4"). After you've banged a girl, assign her a new 6–10 rating based on how much you want to bang her again (ex: "Peaches Davao 9"). Even if you don't bang a girl again (or don't bang her period), save her number so you don't accidentally end up meeting up with her when you don't want to.

It sounds ridiculous, but if you're trying to stick your dick in as many Filipinas as possible, your phone's contact list will be a complete mess unless you organize it somehow. For example, at the end of my first week in the Philippines, I had over *30* girls' numbers in my phone… and that was just girls in one city! By categorizing girls straight off the bat, you'll save yourself a mountain of problems.

Long-Term Dating and Marriage

Once you've banged a girl out, particularly in a conservative city like Davao, you'll have her wrapped around your finger. You're free to see her as often as you like or drop her from your rotation entirely. Don't use this as an excuse to go soft, however. She may be sweet and nurturing, but she still has an inner predator, and if you expose your fleshy underbelly, she'll have no qualms about ripping you apart.

There are only two major problems with dating a Filipina long-term. The first is that they rarely if ever use birth control, due to the sway that Catholicism has over the government and culture. Abortion is also illegal in the Philippines, so any girl you knock up will almost assuredly be keeping the baby. Indeed, I became suspicious that some of the girls I was banging were *trying* to get pregnant so they could have a half-white baby, who would have a leg up in life due to the country's race-based social structure. More than one girl outright told me that if I got them pregnant, they would keep the baby without telling me. I'm still not sure whether that's a compliment or an insult, but I was more comfortable with this arrangement then I otherwise would be because I knew these girls would make great mothers.

As a result, whenever you bang a Filipino girl, you need to be prepared for the possibility that you might impregnate her. While I initially used condoms when I was in Davao, I eventually got lazy and started doing girls raw, blasting on their tits, faces and occasionally in their pussies. STDs really weren't a concern because the girls I was dealing with were sexually inexperienced, a few being virgins. In Manila, I began wrapping it up again because of the higher mean sluttiness of that city's womenfolk. As I mentioned earlier, the U.S. and the Philippines don't have a child support extradition treaty, so if you put a baby in some broad, you can welsh on your parental responsibilities by leaving the country. Even still, I'd advise you to avoid impregnating any girl you're not interested in settling down with.

The second issue with Filipinas is that if you're dating one from a more conservative area, she's eventually going to push for commitment, either in the form of a relationship or marriage. Coming from the gladiatorial arena that is dating in the U.S., I was grateful to meet girls who eager to show me how much they cared. In fact, as I've mentioned already, don't be surprised if some girls—particularly inexperienced ones—tell you that they love you within a few dates. While it's possible to string girls along, the longer you're with one particular girl, the clingier and more possessive she'll get, particularly if she's browner-/more Asian-looking.

I can't lecture you on how to treat the girls that you bang; that's up to you. But I will say this: be careful about leading girls on when you have no interest in settling down with them. If you're in a long-term relationship with a girl, don't casually dismiss her or her feelings. Strong male-female relationships are rare, even more so in the West, and some mistakes can't be undone. The reason why this book is subtitled "How to Make Love with Filipino Girls" as opposed to "How to Bang Filipino Girls" is because love *is* possible with Filipinas, and it's not something you should throw away so easily.

While I wish I could provide more specific game pointers for dealing with Filipinas, the reality is that you don't need them. The Philippines is one of the few countries on Earth where you're best served by following your masculine instincts, and one where you'll be rewarded for doing so. Whether your goal is to slay as many chicks until your dick is about to fall off or find your one true love, you can do it in the Philippines.

IV

CITY GUIDES

Manila

Manila (or, more specifically, Metro Manila) is the capital of the Philippines and its largest city. It's the most tourist-heavy city in the country (outside of possibly Angeles City, which I haven't visited), so your exotic factor isn't nearly as high as it is elsewhere, but the girls compensate by being looser and sluttier. The various component cities and districts of Metro Manila run the gamut from glitzy and wealthy (Makati, Quezon City), sleazy and run-down (Pasay) and everything in between.

The biggest advantage of Manila is that you'll never run out of things to see and do. As the country's capital, most of the Philippines' cultural treasures are located there, such as Rizal Park (an urban park founded atop the place where José Rizal was executed), Intramuros (the oldest district of the city, founded by the Spanish in 1571), Fort

Santiago, and the Malacañang Palace (the residence of the Philippine president). As I mentioned in the opening chapter, there are also plenty of museums and tourist attractions, such as the National Museum of the Philippines, the Ayala Museum, the Museum of the Filipino People, and the Manila Zoo. Finally, Manila has two of the best malls I've ever been in: Greenbelt and the Mall of Asia. Greenbelt is a luxuriously decadent upscale mall in Makati centered around a huge pool full of tropical fish, while the Mall of Asia is the 11th largest mall in the world and even sports its own *ice skating rink*.

Manila's major downsides are its cost of living, cluttered nature and the mentality of the people there. While still considerably cheaper than anywhere in the West, you'll need around $1,500 a month to live comfortably in Manila. Additionally, the city's pollution, traffic, and bum problems will wear on you very quickly. Finally, the sheer number of people trying to hustle you, whether its taxi drivers jamming you for an extra 100 pesos, freelancers offering "boom-boom" for cash, or street urchins panhandling as you walk down the street, gets tiresome after a while. I'm fortunate in that I visited Manila after I'd already been in the country for two months, giving me a strong handle on Philippine culture; if I'd come to the city straight off the bat, I'd likely have been overwhelmed.

Overall, while I recommend stopping by Manila for at least *part* of your Philippine vacation, you really need to get out of the city in order to experience the best parts of the country. Manila provides fun stuff to do, great nightlife, and easy girls for the picking, but it's not somewhere I'd settle down for the long haul.

For lodging, I recommend getting an apartment in either Makati or the Fort (also known as Bonifacio Global City). These are the wealthiest parts of Metro Manila, and by extension the safest. Having a nice apartment in a nice part of town will also help you seal the deal with girls. Quezon City, on the northern end of Metro Manila, is also a safe place to live, but its relative distance from other parts of the city makes logistics kind of a pain.

When it comes to day game, the best places I've found to meet girls are Rizal Park, Greenbelt, and the Mall of Asia. Rizal Park attracts many tourists from around the Philippines due to its importance in the country's history, and it's often packed on Sundays and national holidays. Greenbelt is an ideal place to go if you're looking to meet whiter Filipinas, while the Mall of Asia attracts a more mixed crowd. There are also numerous other malls throughout the city where you can ply your trade. Word to the wise: avoid Harrison Plaza in Pasay, because it's a run-down shithole. In fact, here's a rule of thumb: if a Philippine mall has "plaza" in the name, it's probably a shithole.

For nightlife, your best bets are to check out Makati and the Fort; they're full of high-to-medium-end bars and clubs. For an edgier experience, check out the clubs in Remedios Circle in the Malate district of Manila proper; they draw a lot of South Korean exchange students. Because bars and clubs in the Philippines tend to go out of business and reopen under new names on a regular basis (due to the owners failing to bribe the right public officials), I can't give specific venue pointers in most cases. Be wary in Malate, as it's where the sex industry in Manila is headquartered. Expect lots of prostitutes, strip clubs and go-go bars.

One venue that I *do* recommend you check out (and is unlikely to ever go out of business) is L.A. Café (also known as Manila Bay Café) in Malate.[7] It's as close as you're ever going to get to the Mos Eisley cantina scene in the original *Star Wars*. It's an entertaining place to go people watching, with cheap beer and live music on the second floor. Be on guard though, because L.A. Café is a notorious hooker hangout; you'll have freelancers descending on you the minute you walk in the door. You can sleep with hookers for free by running traditional game on them; most of them are so sick of hooking up with fat, old men that they'll gladly get fucked by a guy they're genuinely attracted to. The secret to L.A. Café is to be firm but pushy when freelancers try to hock their wares. You can also visit Café Havana in Greenbelt for a similar atmosphere (albeit more high-class). I don't recommend hanging around these scummy venues for very long, but they're worth stepping foot into just to see them.

Davao City

If Manila is the New York City of the Philippines, Davao is the Des Moines. Quiet, sleepy and secluded, its atmosphere is completely unlike Manila's. While the city's nightlife is pathetic, the lack of foreigners combined with the city's more conservative ethos makes it an ideal place to find a wife or long-term girlfriend. As I mentioned already, Davao is aided by the fact that it's easily the safest city in the Philippines, with the lowest crime rate and the least corrupt public officials in the country. Even the people there are honest and upright, and beggars are a rare sight on the streets.

The main downside of Davao is that there's not much to do outside of bang girls. The city has a number of malls, most notably Gaisano Mall and Abreeza, but there's little in the way of touristy attractions. Fortunately, the city compensates by being relatively cheap: you can easily get by on about $1,000 a month there. Davao's relatively serene weather (by Philippine standards) is also a plus; the city rarely if ever is hit by typhoons.

Overall, Davao is definitely worth visiting, but make sure you can entertain yourself when you're not hanging out with girls. The city is an ideal place to settle down if you plan to find a girlfriend or wife.

For lodging, you'll want to get an apartment close to the city center. While Davao is very spread out, the actual downtown district is very small, centered on Gaisano and Abreeza malls. Try and find a place in that vicinity, because otherwise you'll spend half your time in taxis stuck in traffic. For example, I stayed at a high-rise that was located about three blocks from Gaisano Mall.

For day game in Davao, your two best options are the aforementioned Gaisano and Abreeza malls. Gaisano attracts a more working-class crowd while Abreeza is more upscale (and has better air conditioning). They're close enough that you can meet girls at one then walk to the other. There's also a smaller mall called Victoria Plaza in between them, but you can skip it. Remember what I said about malls that have "plaza" in the name? There are also a pair of really nice SM brand malls on opposite edges of the city; they're out of the way compared to Gaisano and Abreeza, but are worth checking out if you like variety.

Nightlife in Davao is centered on the intersection of J.P. Laurel Ave. and F. Torres St.[8] This is where you'll find the bulk of the city's bars; in fact, you could theoretically hit them all in a night or two. I really didn't bother with nightlife after my first week in Davao, so I can't help you much here.

Unlike with Manila, girls in Davao will want to know why you're there, since the city doesn't draw a lot of tourist traffic. If girls ask you why you're in town, tell them that you're a businessman; if they're extra persistent, tell them you're looking to open a call center. This should suffice nine times out of ten. Davao girls are more open and trusting than Manila girls, so they won't ruthlessly interrogate you if they happen to like you.

As I've said already, Davao's conservative culture means you're unlikely to get any one-night stands, or even bang girls on the first date. You'll also run into stronger last minute resistance when the time to make the beast with two backs finally comes. Just be patient and persistent. The girls you meet are looking for a man to sweep them off their feet: it's your mission to be that man.

V

FINAL THOUGHTS

The Philippines is chock-full of demure, feminine girls who appreciate strong, charming foreigners. Even the biggest urban slut machine of Manila is more nurturing and caring than the average American woman. My time in the Philippines was the only time in my life where I was getting laid so much—with so many different women—that I became sick of it. It almost felt like a job: texting girls, going on dates, and charming them into taking their clothes off. Much like playing a video game on easy mode, the lack of challenge started to bore me. The only limit to how many girls I could smash was how much abuse my dick could take. When I departed Manila for Chicago at the end of my trip, I was a little *relieved* that I wouldn't have to keep going through the rigmarole of banging Filipinas.

At the same time, because I got so much action in the Philippines—and met so many wonderful girls—the trip changed me for the better. As corny as this sounds, living in the Philippines helped me become a more empathetic man, better able to relate to women, and inspired me to be less of an asshole. I realized that the personality traits I'd adopted to get laid in the U.S. were the result of me adapting to a sick society, one in which men and women have been driven apart by consumerism, cultural Marxism, and moral degeneracy. Living in the Philippines let me experience normality, a world where men and women actually *like* and *cherish* one another.

The biggest downside of my Philippine trip is that it permanently ruined my ability to deal with American girls. When you've spent an entire summer eating expensive steak, how can you even tolerate the taste of a Big Mac? In my first month back in the States, having to witness American girls' bloated egos, atrophied social skills, and antisocial behavior put me in a depression. While the grass isn't *perfectly* green on the other side, the American lawn is so sickly and full of weeds that it's impossible to tolerate once you've gotten a taste of life outside its borders.

At the end of the day, while I did some things over there that I regret, I wouldn't take my adventure in the Philippines back for a second. Filipino girls taught me that there is a world where men and women can form genuine connections and love each other without Marxist social engineering and consumerism getting in the way. They helped bring out a more honest and tender side of my personality.

FINAL THOUGHTS

While your Philippine vacation may not be the eye-opening mindfuck that it was for me, you won't ever regret visiting this great land. Whether you're looking to plow your way through miles of snapper, settle down and start a family, or simply experience what it's like to date normal, feminine women, the Philippines has something to offer you.

Best of luck on your journey.

ENDNOTES

1. Wike, Richard, Bruce Stokes, and Jacob Poushter. "America's Global Image." *Pew Research Center.* Pew Research Center, 23 June 2015. Web. 16 Dec. 2015.
2. V, Roosh. "The Correct Way to Catch a Metered Taxi in South America." *Roosh V.* Roosh V, 17 July 2009. Web. 16 Dec. 2015.
3. Iknowexactly. "Even I Couldn't Fail in the Philippines." *Roosh V Forum.* Roosh V, 21 Mar. 2014. Web. 16 Dec. 2015.
4. Jack, Nicholas. "Ultimate Philippines Data Sheet: Manila, Cebu, Davao, Cagayan De Oro, GenSan, Butuan." *Roosh V Forum.* Roosh V, 19 Feb. 2013. Web. 16 Dec. 2015.
5. Jack, Nicholas. "How I Fucked 19 Pinay Girls in 14 Days in the Philippines." *Swoop the World.* Nicholas Jack, 19 May 2014. Web. 16 Dec. 2015.
6. Fisto. "How to Bang 3 Philippine Girls a Day." *Swoop the World.* Nicholas Jack, 08 July 2013. Web. 16 Dec. 2015.

7. Zolo, Mark. "Manila City Guide." *Naughty Nomad.* Mark Zolo, 28 Apr. 2010. Web. 16 Dec. 2015.
8. Emh. "Davao, Philippines Data Sheet." *Roosh V Forum.* Roosh V, 29 Feb. 2011. Web. 16 Dec. 2015.

ABOUT THE AUTHOR

Matt Forney was born in 1988 in Rome, New York and grew up in nearby Syracuse. A graduate of Christian Brothers Academy, he later attended SUNY Plattsburgh and the University at Albany, majoring in English and journalism. A former retail wage slave, bureaucrat and ditch-digger, Matt began writing under his real name in 2012 to chronicle a hitchhiking trip he took from Syracuse to Portland, Oregon.

Matt's writing has been published at *Return of Kings, Taki's Magazine, Right On, Alternative Right, The Spearhead* and many other sites. He also served as the editor of *Reaxxion,* a gaming website for men.

For more info about Matt, go to his website, *MattForney.com.*